Barry Fantoni, novelist, broadcaster, jazz musician, reviewer, illustrator, film and TV actor, *Private Eye* contributor, *The Times* diary cartoonist, was born on February 28, 1940.

Look at Page 44 at the bottom of paragraph 2.

Weird eh ?

Happy b'day!

Love Matt 3/2/89

Barry Fantoni's Chinese Horoscopes

THE HORSE

SPHERE BOOKS LIMITED

SPHERE BOOKS LIMITED

Penguin Books Ltd, 27 Wrights Lane, London W8 5TZ (Publishing and Editorial)
and Harmondsworth, Middlesex, England (Distribution and Warehouse)
Viking Penguin Inc., 40 West 23rd Street, New York, New York 10010, USA
Penguin Books Australia Ltd, Ringwood, Victoria, Australia
Penguin Books Canada Ltd, 2801 John Street, Markham, Ontario, Canada L3R 1B4
Penguin Books (NZ) Ltd, 182–190 Wairau Road, Auckland 10, New Zealand

First published in Great Britain by Sphere Books Ltd 1987

Made and printed in Great Britain by
Richard Clay Ltd, Bungay, Suffolk
Filmset in 9½/10pt Photina

To my family of Roosters

Acknowledgements

I should like to express my thanks to all those many friends, relatives and strangers who have both knowingly and otherwise helped with the compilation of this book. I should like to thank in particular Gillian Jason who researched the beautiful Chinese illustrations, The British Library for granting permission to reproduce them, and Dr Hin Hung Ho for the delightful calligraphy. But the bulk of my gratitude is reserved for my Rooster wife who ploughed on relentlessly with the list of celebrities whose names are scattered throughout, and without which this book could never have been written.

Introduction

How do you introduce yourself? Do you first give your name, or say what school you went to, or where you live, or what kind of job you do? Whatever you say, the chances are that you will be attempting in some small way to summarise who you imagine yourself to be, and hoping that the label you choose will do the *real* you justice.

In the East, however, introductions may take on a very different form. Because of a system that has evolved throughout Eastern civilisation, everyone has a birth sign named after one of the twelve animals that make up the Chinese Horoscope. Consequently, when two strangers meet, instead of giving their names, they might well refer to their animal sign. 'I am a Horse,' one might say.

'Pleased to meet you,' might come the reply, 'I am a Tiger.'

As a result of this simple greeting, a great deal of unspoken information will have changed hands. In that particular case, if they had met to discuss business, both Horse and Tiger will probably have parted on good terms. However, if the Tiger had been another Horse I suspect that the two Chinese businessmen would have given the meeting a miss. And for a very good reason. For the Peoples of the East, an individual's personal animal sign, dictated by the year of birth, plays a central role in the conduct of their daily lives. Since I was introduced to the system some thirteen years ago, it has revolutionised mine. Chinese horoscopes have shown me a completely fresh way of viewing human behaviour, one that can be of great practical use. It can, for example, guide us to the best business associate, help us in our choice of marriage partners and even suggest the ideal lover. Chinese Horoscopes tell us why we dress like we do, why some of us save every penny while others spend without caring. We learn why some are content to sit at home while others travel to the four corners of the globe. It explains who we really are, not only to the world at large, but more importantly to ourselves.

No one is certain how the Chinese Horoscope first came into being, but there is, as with all mysteries, a legend which I believe makes up in poetical charm what it lacks in scientific probability.

Five centuries before the birth of Christ, so the legend has it, the Buddha sent out an invitation to all the animals in his Kingdom, asking if they would join him in the New Year celebrations. For reasons that seem only known to the animals themselves, only twelve turned up. In order of arrival there came: the rat, the buffalo, the tiger, the cat, the dragon, the snake, the horse, the goat, the monkey, the rooster, the dog and last of all the pig. Cheered by their presence, the Buddha decided to show his gratitude by honouring each animal with a year, calling it by their name. Moreover, all people born in that year would inherit the animal's characteristics. Horses would be graceful and practical, Dogs would be anxious and loyal. Unlike Western astrology which is based on the movement of the sun and the stars, the Chinese use the lunar cycle. There are twelve moons in a lunar cycle, plus an extra moon every thirteen (our Blue Moon), which is why the Chinese New Year never falls on the same day. So, with twelve moons and twelve animals there evolved a perfect pattern. Heaven alone knows what would have happened if a few camels and ducks had decided to show up for the Buddha's party!

Given such an explanation, the most obvious question for us Western sceptics to ask is how on earth can all those born in the same year inherit the same characteristics? The answer is of course that we are not all identical. And it was only when I had stopped asking that same question about the thousands of people I didn't know, asking instead if it were true of myself, that I discovered that the system of Chinese Horoscopes really worked. Testing the system first on my own sign, then on my family and friends, and finally on a large number of celebrities whose lives I am familiar with, I was left in no doubt that it was startlingly accurate. In other words, instead of generalising, I looked at specific cases. And once I had shed my scepticism I began to understand more clearly the Chinese view of the twelve animal signs, and the influence they exercise over our lives.

The sign of our parents, the sign of marriage and business partners and the signs of our children all create variations on the way our own animal sign influences us. The eager to please Dragon son will benefit enormously from his adoring Rooster mother, while the passionate Rat will find the anxious Dog impervious to her advances. Time of birth is another factor which determines a subtle difference in temperament. Goats born in the summer will be less capricious than those born in winter, whereas Snakes born during a sudden thunderstorm will be in danger all their lives.

This book gives an idea of the markedly different attitudes between the two cultures of East and West. To seek pleasure and enjoyment from life is an inherent part of Chinese philosophy. The West on the other hand, frowns on those who treat life like a game. The East recognises that the games we play, both as adults and children, are a form of make-believe which not only enhances life but in some mysterious way offers us the key to true self-discovery. The West puts men on the Moon, the East puts men in touch with their real selves; or in other words, the animal within.

Clearly no one can foretell our destiny, and even if one could, so many conflicting factors would make escaping it an absolute impossibility. The Chinese Horoscope has little or nothing to do with the Western signs of the Zodiac. What it teaches is not a plan for tomorrow, but a way to know yourself today and every day. To learn who we are through our influencing animal is to take part in a wonderful ancient game that will make our lives both richer and happier.

Barry Fantoni's
Chinese Horoscopes

THE HORSE

1906*	January 25th to February 12th	**1907**
1918	February 11th to January 31st	**1919**
1930	January 30th to February 16th	**1931**
1942	February 15th to February 4th	**1943**
1954	February 3rd to January 23rd	**1955**
1966*	January 21st to February 8th	**1967**
1978	February 7th to January 27th	**1979**
1990	January 27th to February 14th	**1991**

* FIRE HORSE

'When I consider the most wonderful work of God in the creation of the Horse, endowing it with a singular body and a noble spirit, the principal whereof is a loving and dutiful inclination to the service of man.'

Topsell

The Year of the Horse

A hectic year with work for everyone who wants it, with few strikes and the minimum industrial unrest. The year of the Horse shows a considerable change from its predecessor; gone are the hours spent in peaceful meditation, and gone too, is the benign wisdom. In the place of spiritualism, we find noble and industrial effort. The Horse year will begin as it means to continue (and end) with an all-pervading spirit of elegance and independence. And although the Horse is universally admired for his industry, he also knows how to enjoy his leisure. As a result, the Horse year will bring about many great sporting achievements with new sports stars setting records which will remain unbroken for decades at a time. In 1954, Roger Bannister set the most significant sporting record in history, by becoming the first man ever to run a mile in under four minutes.

The year of the Horse will also be noted for the many political changes taking place, mostly following the collapse or the overthrow of kings and presidents. The month of November 1918 witnessed the abdication of the Kaiser, and in 1978 Mrs Gandhi was expelled from the Indian parliament. The Horse is seldom far from the political arena, but when in control he makes few dramatic changes. Those he does make will be slight, and always for the best.

Horse years tend to provide us with optimism for our many projects and there will be a general atmosphere of good humour. There will, of course, be the odd black moment, and even serious conflict, but it will not last. However bloody, confrontations will fizzle out, sometimes in a matter of weeks, sometimes days, or even in a matter of hours. Mrs Gandhi spent only six days in prison. However, wars, famines and pestilences are not so lenient in the year of the Fire Horse. Occurring every sixty years (1906 was a Fire Horse year, so was 1966), the Chinese believe that whatever happens in the year of the Fire Horse, both good and bad, will be intensified many times over. San Francisco was destroyed by an earth-quake in 1906, and in 1666 London was burnt to the ground. In the first nine months of 1966 airline disasters accounted for a record number of 460 lives lost, and in July of the same year, England won the World Cup, beating Germany 4-2 with goals that are still disputed.

Love will hit hard in the year of the Horse, and hit quickly. And love should be allowed its freedom. Above all, the year will contain an air of expectancy throughout, and there will be a constant promise of life looking up. In 1954, the London gold market re-opened after a closure of fifteen years.

In the year of the Horse we will all adapt more easily to shifts in circumstances, and the way to proceed is not by sitting for hours in deep contemplation, but by chancing your arm. And don't be afraid of taking advice; remember that the best advice you can get is straight from the Horse's mouth.

The Horse is born under the twin signs of elegance and ardour

The Horse Personality

---

*'Time to be out and about,
seeing new places, meeting new people;
let the elegant Horse be your guide.'*

Of all the animals on earth, there can be no doubt that the
graceful Horse, with his inner spirit of freedom, is by far the
most popular. Certainly no creature has worked harder, or
longer, for Mankind. Whether it's the majestic stallions from
the Vienna riding stables, or the delightful shaggy-maned
Shetland ponies that carry our children so obediently across
the summer beaches, every one of us has our favourite. And
there are so many horses from which we can make our choice;
Arabian thoroughbreds, show jumpers, pit ponies, hunters,
plough pullers, steeple-chasers, flat racers, mountain trekkers,
cab horses, cart horses, dray horses, donkeys, mules, asses –
all part of one enormous equine family. And the seemingly
infinite variety of skills, shapes and sizes are also to be found
in all those born under the Horse's powerful influence.

A strongly masculine sign, both male and female Horses
brim over with personality. Easy-going, the Horse has a
natural flair for leadership and will be found at the heart of
any gathering. Horse women in particular are strikingly
beautiful, and are frequently seen captivating an ever present
band of admirers with their witty observations and brilliant
chat. And should a Horse lady lack just a little in looks, she'll
make up for it in sheer style, of that you may be absolutely
certain. Her hair will have been cut in the very latest 'in'

salon, her shoes will have Italian design written all over them, and her perfume will have cost her half a year's salary. No other creature is as beautiful and witty as Ms Horse in her best form. Sorry, gals, but that's how it is.

Male horses are conspicuous by the strength of their personality, as well as their good looks, and many have an instant sex appeal. Aware of his powers, the Horse does not brag, although it must be said right at the start that the Horse can be very vain. If you were born under the sign of the Horse, the following will be kindred spirits; Paul McCartney, Clint Eastwood, Barbra Streisand, Billy Connolly, Chopin, Lord Snowdon, Princess Margaret and Sean Connery.

Born under the sign of elegance and endurance, the Horse is noted for his highly original sense of humour. He is also extremely practical, and his industry knows few peers. What is more, the Horse's natural sense of public ease and his great inner reserves mark him for the very highest posts in public life. He can address crowds of thousands as if he were having a chat to a chum in the pub. The evangelist Billy Graham, is a Horse, as is Shirley Williams.

One of the central reasons why a Horse is so successful is to be found in his great capacity to work round the clock when the occasion demands it. Indeed, it must be said that Horses do work very odd hours, and you'll often find them packing up just as you start, and turning up just as you are about to go home. But however many hours a Horse works, he'll still approach every problem put before him with a clear head, and solve it with a sharp decisive mind. And to add another string to the Horse's already overloaded bow, he is capable of working methodically and speedily, seeing the job on hand through to the end. When there's work to be done, you'll not find the Horse hanging around in the canteen; that comes later.

I have a friend who is a Horse, and worked for many years as a journalist on *The Sunday Times*. He thought nothing of flying off at a minute's notice to one of the world's trouble spots with nothing more than an overnight bag and his wits to enable him to get his story. Each assignment would always present the same string of problems: first he would have to find accommodation (often in some godforsaken dot on the map), an interpreter, a telephone, transport to the scene of the action, contacts, informers, other journalists, and so on. After getting his story, he'd write it, send it to the newspaper over the wire and, if he was lucky, get back to London in time to check the proofs before the paper was finally put to bed. As an important member of the *Insight* team, Peter Gillman was a key figure in compiling the special reports investigated by *Insight* and turning them into instant paperbacks. His record here is impressive, even by the high standards of the Horse. On the book about the Iranian Embassy siege, he wrote no less than 24,000 words in *four days*! And for *The Sunday Times'* book on the Falklands war, he wrote 30,000 words in fourteen days. But journalist Horses are not the only ones who can churn it out. Didn't that most brilliant and original of all British humorists, Spike Milligan, write one Goon Show script a week for over a decade? It's just as well that the Horse has been endowed with more than his fair share of stamina.

Because the Horse is capable of making a decision quickly, without fuss and, more often than not, without error, he makes a formidable opponent on the political rostrum. Lenin, Krushchev and Leonid Brezhnev were born in the Year of the Horse. So was Neil Kinnock.

One quite astonishing power that a Horse possesses is his ability to grasp the point you are about to make almost before you have even begun to make it. There are times when he will finish your sentence, and do so more eloquently than you would have done yourself. This is not necessarily a question of a sixth sense, or indeed, horse sense. It is, quite simply, a case of the Horse's logical mind. In other words, if what you are telling a Horse makes sense, he'll get the point without the frills. He might like embellishment, but the Horse doesn't really need it. And be warned. If you expect the Horse to take you seriously, do not jabber on. Nothing is guaranteed to irritate him more, and the Horse who is irritated by gibberish will show his feelings openly. Be prepared to be ridiculed. And it will fare even worse if you cross him in debate with some half thought out nonsense. In such an instance you might actually send the Horse into a rage. Although he is not easily vexed, the Horse's anger is something to fear. And once you have been on the receiving end, you will never forget it. Even though he is quick to apologise for what are often rather child-like tantrums, you will never view the Horse in quite the same way again. You will certainly feel less easy in his company. I am sure that riders who have been thrown by a rearing Horse know the feeling.

As a rule, Horses are not jealous or possessive about those they love and do not impose double standards. They require their freedom, and realise that their partners expect the same. But the Horse likes to have his own way. And one sure way to get him riled is to cross him in public – which I suspect brings us back to Lenin and Co. Remarkably calm in a crisis, the Horse will seldom put his view forward unless he is absolutely certain of his facts. Whether discussing cricket averages, political history, or some off-beat pastime like bee-keeping, the Horse will never quote you a wrong statistic or give you a woolly-minded opinion. For all his high spirits, wit, and free and easy manner, the Horse is above all a practical creature. He deals in facts, not opinions. And should he make the occasional error, as we all do, the Horse's practical approach will be a useful tool to help talk his way out of trouble. He can sound convincing even when he's barking completely up the wrong tree.

The male Horse is a really tough guy to win over, and if that is your intention, steer well clear of topics that introduce an element of mysticism – Zen Buddhism, reincarnation and zodiacs. The way to win his interest is by a well-informed dissertation on mountaineering, French wines or how to plumb in your own solar energy system. If all else fails you can always hook a Horse with a little scurrilous gossip. Horses like to stick their long necks over the five bar gate, and far too many of them find that they are given secrets they cannot be trusted to keep. They also talk too much. But Horses are not generally speaking judgemental, and are most willing to accept faults in others, passing them off with a shrug. They are however, extremely competitive.

With a practical mind and ability to adapt his moods to suit the situation, the Horse can and does take on a number of professional roles. When one considers the huge variation of jobs that man has given the horse, it is easy to understand why no door is really closed to him.

No matter whether the gathering is large or small, the Horse loves company and is an inveterate party thrower. To put it to the test, my wife and I drew up a separate list of our favourite party throwers. Marks were given for interesting guests, food and wine and the general standard of hospitality. A Horse featured in the first three places, with a double Horse partnership passing the post by a short head. My feelings are that if you can spare five minutes to draw up your own top host and hostess list, you too will find a Horse with his or her head in the frame every time.

Although fiercely independent, one of the Horse's most endearing qualities is his way of asking for advice, even when it might well concern deeply personal aspects of his private life. Unlike the Monkey, say, who will trick advice from you, the Horse will take you quietly to one side and come straight out with it. He will listen carefully, weighing up in his own mind what you are saying. Whether he takes it or not, whether he acts on either your good or bad advice, the Horse will go to some considerable lengths to show his gratitude. But however he rewards you, he will never forget your concern.

If it appears on the surface that Horses have got everything going for them, it must be remembered that they often face troubled times when caught in the web of romance. Horses fall in love at the drop of the proverbial hat and can do very little to counter such blows to the heart. With his great sex appeal, good looks and personality, any advances he cares to make will, in almost all cases, meet with little resistance. In the case of a lady Horse, she will have an endless string of offers, and fortunately or unfortunately, depending on the circumstances, she will not find herself very often saying, 'no'. Although they don't get bitter and twisted when love doesn't work out in the way they had expected (Horses do have very high standards of love-making), they do nevertheless have a tough time coming to terms with love's sharper angles. Because the Horse is so practical, he'll attempt to reason love out. But love cannot be reasoned and the Horse will frequently become confused, and ultimately disillusioned. What is worse, in matters of the heart the Horse never learns from his or her mistakes. He thinks that every affair is the one that will last, and therefore throws himself at it hammer and tongs. Alas, for all of us, we can make many mistakes before choosing the partner who will suit us best, but the Horse has more trouble than most in making that choice. Consequently the Horse may often marry many times before finding Mr or

Mrs Right. But when you have experienced a Horse's love – the female Horse is so stimulating – the chances are that you will never forget it. As one very worldwise Dragon friend once admitted to me about his Horse wife: 'She's the most *exciting* person I have ever known.'

Because the Lady Horse very often has the kind of looks that put her on the covers of the world's glossy fashion magazines, she very often knows how to dress in the latest thing, looking neither outrageously trendy, nor as so many do, a little silly. Born under the sign of the Horse, Jean Shrimpton was the most talked about fashion model for almost two decades, and her beauty and individuality created a set of ideals about the nature of young women's looks which apply even today. If the latest thing is a boiler suit and stiletto heels, the Horse will be wearing them before anyone else. And if tomorrow's in-thing looks ghastly, on a Horse it will look great. And if you want to know what the latest in hairstyles is, look up your Horse friend. Horses are very conscious about their manes and tails, and grooms spend no end of time fussing over them.

Male Horses display a different attitude to the way they dress, and their wardrobe will be full of straightforward clothes that hang easily. Although he might wear a bright neck-tie or buy expensive shoes, the Horse will never overdress. He likes to feel relaxed and comfortable. Unless his job demands it, the Horse is not likely to own a dinner jacket. As much as he loves social gatherings, he prefers the less formal kind, but he will always dress with distinction, allowing his great individuality full reign.

Because the Horse is so adaptable, he is also likely to change his life more than most; some might argue that the Horse is in fact a victim of change. And it is true that in addition to sometimes changing his wife (or her husband), the Horse does seem to be constantly jumping from one job, hobby, interest and pastime to another. It can be very confusing to learn that the chap you have known as a do-it-yourself winemaker has now started to learn Urdu, or the woman who worked as a fashion editor has become one of Mother Teresa's helpers. Much worse follows when you discover that whereas last week you were the most divine thing ever to have crossed the Horse's path, she can now hardly recall your name, let alone your telephone number. And for all their practicality, Horses do not plan for the long term. When they want something, they must have it at once. Do not try to prevent a Horse achieving his aim by standing idly in the way. He'll stampede over you as if you didn't exist.

The Horse's home will be a mixture of comfort and refined taste. The accent will always be on simplicity, but the practical side of the Horse will express itself in that he will buy quality, seeing no sense in spending money on sofas that will collapse in five minutes, or carpets that won't stand more than a week's wear. And there will be many touches of the Horse's individuality, perhaps in the choice of pictures that hang from uncluttered walls, or the colour of the furnishing fabrics. And there will always be plenty to eat in a Horse's home – the Horse can get his gnashers through a meadow in no time at all.

The Horse is an extremely practical animal who, for reasons only known to Horses, becomes quickly bored. The last kind of holiday a Horse should consider is one which involves the same old routine every day – breakfast, beach, dinner, disco. A Horse treasures his independence above all else – his freedom to roam is crucial to his well being. An active vacation is advised, one which involves more than just getting a tan. The best plan for a British Horse is to keep out of the Horse box and spend as little time as possible travelling, unless it's on foot. A walking tour of the Scottish Highlands is perfect. Failing that, a sailing holiday off the Norfolk Broads.

Because his love of freedom is paramount to a Horse, it will largely determine the three phases of his life. Horse children very often leave home at an early age, finding even the most well-meaning of parental control a restriction. The middle period will be mixed, with the Horse's constant changing about acting against his better interests. However, old age sits comfortably on a Horse's shoulders, and even though, as in the case of Neil Armstrong, he has been to the moon and back, the Horse will be quite content to roam around the lush pasture, dream of his many fillies, mares and victories, and watch the world go by. The Chinese say that the Horse born in the summer has an easier life than a Horse born in the winter. If that is the case, no one is better able at reversing his lot than the Horse. Absolutely no one.

Horse as Parent

The Horse automatically becomes the key figure of any family circle, yet he is sometimes more keen on life at the office than he is with his wife and kids. Perhaps it has something to do with the Horse's great need for independence. However, the Horse is great with his children once he actually decides to come home, but he isn't always over-amused by the young Rat. Horse fathers want to see their sons in a skilled trade, not raiding the tea caddy on the mantelpiece. The baby Buffalo fares marginally better in the Horse house, but here it's a case of too much study. Stamp collecting is OK in its place, but the Horse loves the sound of laughter now and again.

The infant Pig will please his mother Horse. He'll giggle and wiggle his toes, but his looks . . . well, couldn't they be just a little more *attractive?* The puppy Dog is such an open-eyed little soul, and so serious. One day he will set the world to rights. Such worthiness, alas, is a bit of a lead balloon in the home of the Horse. The young Rooster son has plenty to say for himself and likes a lark. His trouble is he has too much to say, and usually in the wrong places. The Kitten will behave herself, though, and make the right kind of noises, but she'll have to do more than purr for her dish of cream.

The Horse father will not understand his Snake son. Why does the child sit around the house all day doing nothing? But the Snake needs his parent's attention and understanding, and will win it in the end, though at some considerable cost. The Dragon child is quite another matter. The Horse parent knows talent when he sees it, and will give the young Dragon all the encouragement he needs. But a Horse mum might tend to mock the Dragon son a little too often – he's so full of himself and she's so quick witted.

There will be no affection shortage in the life of a young Tiger if his parent is a Horse, and the Tiger daughter will be steadied by the firm hand of a Horse father. The Goat daughter makes her intentions clear from the very start; freedom to do her own thing is what she wants, and lots of it. That won't worry the Horse mother, who is herself a libertine at heart and no hypocrite. The baby Monkey is a quick learner and will be much admired under the Horse's roof. Her skills won't be overlooked and so long as she remembers that the Horse is boss in his own home, everything will turn out fine. But *will* she remember?

The business of head of the family will present the Horse child with a problem. The stallion will be in constant conflict with his father, and although the bond between Horses is very strong indeed, they sometimes find expressing family ties difficult. As is so very often the case, the young colt will make an early departure.

Compatibility of Horse Parent and Child

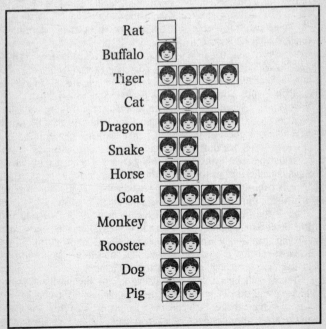

Rat
Buffalo
Tiger
Cat
Dragon
Snake
Horse
Goat
Monkey
Rooster
Dog
Pig

Horse in Business

Each animal in the Chinese horoscope has one polar opposite – creatures who can see eye to eye on absolutely nothing. In the case of the Horse, it is the opportunist Rat. The Horse demands a practical mind from those he works with, not sharp salesmanship. Two Horses on the board of directors have an equally poor chance of agreeing. Their problem is one of practicality, not when a deal should be struck, but how? The Pig is dependable, and puts the hours in. But he is ambitious beneath his cloak of joviality, and the Horse won't like too many fingers in his pie, not at management level. The Cat has the kind of slow and methodical approach to work that the Horse finds he can handle. But the Cat must make sure he doesn't fuss too much.

The Buffalo will make a splendid partner for the Horse. His ability to toil under pressure mirrors the Horse's own great capacity for endurance. The Horse will flatter the Buffalo to keep him happy, but is that always wise? The artistic Goat will work happily and faithfully under a Horse, and will benefit from the Horse's high-powered and positive approach. But the Goat must stick at it, and not talk too much about how well their rivals are doing. An even better partnership is that formed by the Horse and the well-organised Rooster, who can always be relied upon to deal with the tricky customer on the phone. A high-class estate agent's is tailor-made for the Horse and Rooster partnership, or possibly a betting shop.

Tigers are people who just love ideas, and Horses love putting them into practice. No problems at all here, except that the Tiger might dry up before they bank their first million. Both Horses and Snakes can get on in a business relationship, but the Horse uses his personality to resolve difficult situations, the Snake uses her intuition. There could be conflict. The loyal Dog will do his share alongside the Horse. Both can lay claim to have worked the hardest for Man, so why not for each other? The only drawback is the Dog's inborn pessimism.

The clever Money can be practical when he wants, as well as industrious. Under the hand of the honest Horse, he might even find he enjoys playing it straight. But the chances that the Monkey will change his ways are slim, and the Horse will not stand for too much double-dealing. The Horse is a great one for changing his plans, even when things are going well. The Dragon is adaptable, and will put up with change, so long as the changes are for the best. Dragons and Horses should go into the film business. As artisan and showman they have few equals.

Compatibility of Horse in Business Relationships

Sign	Rating
Rat	(none)
Buffalo	💰💰💰💰
Tiger	💰💰💰💰💰
Cat	💰💰💰💰
Dragon	💰💰💰💰
Snake	💰💰💰
Horse	(none)
Goat	💰💰💰💰
Monkey	💰
Rooster	💰💰💰💰💰
Dog	💰💰💰
Pig	(none)

Horse in Love

The Horse is not exactly a fickle romancer, it is just that he falls in love easily, and often. In fact, when a Horse is hit by one of those little arrows Cupid fires, he gets hit good and hard. But a Horse enjoys love, and generally speaking can handle it quite well, for all the heartache. The amorous Pig is also one to give his heart quickly. But Pigs look for security in love, which is something that the freedom-loving Horse can never provide. The old-fashioned Rooster wants a total commitment from her lover, and once again the Horse will be found wanting. The Monkey in love with the Horse will fare even less well. The Monkey *is* a fickle creature whose love-making can very often be both transparently one-sided and insincere. This can only have a negative effect on the Horse. Pigs, Roosters and Monkeys will never enjoy the Horse's love, and for all concerned, perhaps it's better that way.

The lady Rat is an irrepressible flirt and does not understand the meaning of fidelity. A short, sharp affair is the most likely outcome with the Horse becoming and more frustrated. The lady Horse might well become attracted to the male Buffalo, admiring his strong will and sense of purpose, but she'll soon grow tired of his unromantic flannel pyjamas, and long, uncomfortable silences. Lady Dogs are not so much romantic as loving, and they adore Big Strong Creatures like the Horse. She'll be *so* anxious to please, she might even stop criticising his every little fault. In return, the Horse will protect the loving Dog.

Two Horses are made for each other. Stallion and Mare will simply sit gazing into their eyes, telling themselves just how lucky they are to have been born so wonderful. Vanity also plays a big part in the romance between a Snake and a Horse. Bewitched by the Snake's mysterious beauty – his is so up front – the Horse will do everything he can to please the ardent reptile. And she'll adore his wit and social ease. But the Horse will show his speed when the Snake begins to coil her body. The sensuous Cat will enjoy the Horse's good humour, as well as his more personal attentions. But she mustn't expect the Horse to fall in with her routine. The Goat has no sense of routine, but a great sense of humour. As lovers the Horse and the Goat will get on terribly well – real harmony. But the Goat must never take the Horse for granted.

The Tiger is always the extrovert in matters of the heart, and the Horse loves action. Again, a fast and furious affair with no regrets at the sudden end. Not one. And when the lady Horse falls for the seductive Dragon, the whole thing will be over even faster. He won't stand for her merciless teasing for more than a night, unless of course she is very beautiful, very witty, and very elegant. In that case the Dragon will be hooked, poor old thing.

Compatibility of Horse in Love

	Hearts
Rat	♡
Buffalo	♡
Tiger	♡♡♡♡
Cat	♡♡♡♡
Dragon	♡♡♡
Snake	♡♡♡♡
Horse	♡♡♡♡♡
Goat	♡♡♡♡♡
Monkey	
Rooster	
Dog	♡♡♡♡♡
Pig	

Horse in Marriage

The Horse is a family man at heart, whatever ideas about himself he might have to the contrary. Once married and settled down, the Horse takes on his responsibilities without fuss and gets on with the job with an admirable self-assurance. A marriage between two Horses is highly recommended. Their easy-going nature will help see them through the bad times and their good humour and attractive looks will make them popular, however life treats them. The sensuous lady Cat will also make a perfect partner for the Horse. She will cope with his likes and dislikes, furnish his home comfortably and flatter him by whispering sweet nothings. The social Goat has every bit as good chance as the Cat to provide the Horse with a perfect marriage partner. Lady Goats have a warm and gentle sense of humour that attracts the Horse, and her gatherings, built around those he most enjoys, will be a talked-about delight. The lady Pig is also a splendid homemaker, but the Horse's independence will suffer just a little when weighed down by all those home-baked chocolate cakes, cheese flans and steak and kidney pies – he'll hardly be able to get up from the table to read the kids a goodnight fairy tale.

Roosters and Horses generally get on very well in married life. Both love the garden, and apart from the occasional mis-understanding with regard to the Horse's pretty young sec-retary, all should run fairly smoothly. The Dog, once wed, will do everything he can to express his loyalty and devotion, and the Horse will not abuse the Dog's open-hearted trust. But the Horse cannot help himself when he falls in love, and so the Dog must not pry too deeply into the Horse's personal affairs. The bewitching Snake is happy for the Horse to dom-inate in most matters, and will make a good partner once the Horse respects her need to keep silent once in a while. But will the Snake respect the Horse's need for independence? A fifty-fifty chance would be too generous.

The Tiger is impetuous, and might become besotted by the

charm and beauty of the female Horse. He'll whisk her off and marry her, and then face the fact that they are both creatures capable of great personal change. The Dragon is easily adaptable, but very full of himself. He might easily fall for the lady Horse in a big way, but she will seldom give the Dragon her devoted attention. Generally speaking Horses and Dragons should avoid marriage, but when it goes well, nothing can stand in the way. Like a rosebed in a drought, the Horse/Dragon marriage will need a great deal of attention.

The Rat will begin married life with a Horse full of good intentions, but he is, like the Horse, easily led. Both know this, but it is not the wisest basis for a marriage. No Rolls at the front gate for the Horse and Buffalo either, if they can avoid it. The Buffalo likes to be the boss at home, and so does

Compatibility with Horse in Marriage

Rat	▢
Buffalo	▢
Tiger	▩▩▩
Cat	▩▩▩▩▩
Dragon	▩▩
Snake	▩▩▩
Horse	▩▩▩▩▩▩
Goat	▩▩▩▩▩▩
Monkey	▢
Rooster	▩▩▩▩
Dog	▩▩▩▩
Pig	▩▩

the Horse. A master cannot have two servants, nor a home two masters. Oh dear.

The Horse and Monkey will not quibble over who wears the trousers, and enjoy each other's jokes, but they will compete day and night for the mirror, and their marriage will end up in conflict of vanities.

Horses are industrious and display a marked independence in everything they do

Princess Margaret
(*Rex Features Ltd*)

Lord Snowdon
(*Rex Features Ltd*)

Samantha Fox
(*Popperfoto*)

Chris Evert
(*Rex Features Ltd*)

Billy Connolly
(*Rex Features Ltd*)

Barbra Streisand
(*Rex Features Ltd*)

Paul McCartney
(*Rex Features Ltd*)

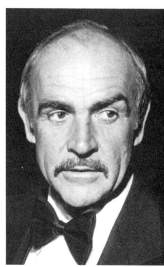

Sean Connery
(*Rex Features Ltd*)

How you will be influenced in the Year of the Horse

A Year for Elegance and Freedom

Of all the twelve signs, only the Horse is not guaranteed good fortune in his own year, and in the year of the Fire Horse it can even be a positive disaster (*see* page 15). But again if the fates smile on the Horse, he will experience unparalleled success, and whatever winds of change blow, will certainly be blowing in his favour. An equally splendid year for the Horse's sometime companion in the meadow, the capricious Goat. Invitations to thrilling parties will come flooding through her letterbox, and should she care to work a little she'll be amply rewarded for her efforts. The Buffalo will also have his work cut out. When the corn is ripe in a Horse year, it grows high and plentiful, but the resolute Buffalo will not complain about the extra hours.

As in all years, Dragons do their own thing and the Horse year will not prevent him from leading his carnival parade. It will, in fact, encourage the spectacle. Like the Goat, the well-mannered Cat will enjoy a full social calender, but don't ask the Cat to go cross-country running. The sensuous Snake will quickly cotton on to the fact that the Horse year is rich with affairs of the heart, but she won't take kindly to all the odd hours the Horse asks her to work. The talkative Rooster adores to be seen in fashionable circles and this year she'll have ample opportunities. And who knows, the Rooster might even let her hair down and have a frolic in the hay. One way or another, a good twelve months for the Rooster, whose bank balance will be in the black for a change. The Tiger will also see an upward trend in his finances, but with so much easy-going romance in the air, the Tiger's volatile heart might find itself overstretched.

The Monkey's gift for hogging the stage will not win him many friends this year and there will be many clashes of vanity. But the artful Monkey will make out; he always does. Trouble for the cheerful Pig, who, in spite of all his hard and honest work, will find the Horse year too much in terms of fickle romance. Pigs like a bit of fun, but they take themselves a trifle seriously when they fall in love. The Dog, so loyal, will find no one takes his devotion at all seriously, or his defenceless trust. But one or two might love him a wee bit; it's that kind of year. As for the opportunist Rat, the charm he uses for his socially mobile life will work against him. Time for the Rat to tighten his belt.

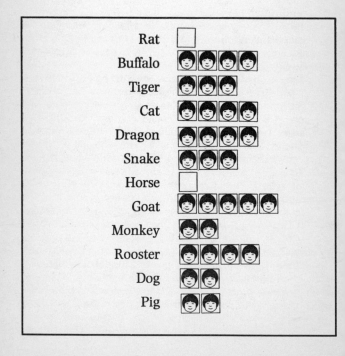

Famous Horses

Spike Milligan

There is something in the nature of all those born in the Year of the Horse that tends to place them at the head of any crowd. Put a Horse in any group and it won't be long before he takes it over, often using little more than the sheer strength of his personality. And one of the many assets that gives the Horse such a social advantage is a lively and intelligent mind. A little vain at times, Horses are nevertheless decisive and stand no nonsense. Both male and female (or should it be mare and stallion?), are nothing if not witty. Because Horses are highly individual, should they choose to use their wit professionally, Horse comics usually emerge as delightfully original. Both Rowan Atkinson and Billy Connolly are Horses. But the Horse who has spanned almost half a century with his utterly unique brand of Horse laughter is Spike Milligan. In his self-created Theatre of the Ridiculous, Mr Milligan, a.k.a Sir Spike Millingoon, Eccles, and a hundred others, has no peer.

Spike Milligan was born in Ahmednagar on April 16, 1918. From the very beginning Spike's life seemed to be an echo of his eccentric humour. His first education took place in a tent in Hyderabad. The young Milligan made his stage debut at his convent school in Poona, aged eight. But whatever he did before, and in spite of his continued brilliance, Spike Milligan will be remembered first and foremost as the inspiration behind *The Goon Show*. For a decade and more, Spike wrote a weekly script. The effort he freely admits drove him mad – literally. To both write and perform at such a demanding level (for millions of fans, *The Goon Show* was a way of life) required tremendous stamina. This, thanks to his Horse influence, Spike had in abundance. But even the most durable of Horses will collapse when pushed beyond their limit. And Spike is no cart Horse.

The Goon Show was unique in the annals of British humour.

A lot had to do with the compatibility of the three central performers, which when viewed through the Chinese Horoscope is more or less perfect. Peter Sellers was a Buffalo, a sign which has nothing in common with a Horse. But the third member of the trio, Harry Secombe, is a Rooster, a sign which nets five stars for compatibility with both Buffalo and Horse. Indeed, when listening to an old *Goon Show* recording, it is impossible to escape the fact that Harry Secombe's role as Neddy Seagoon serves as a catalyst for Peter and Spike. He draws the quite different comic styles of Horse and Buffalo into the open and gives them free rein.

Because of the Horse's practical streak, he is able to get to the heart of the matter on hand faster than most. And when something is out of line, he can spot it at once – Horse sense, you might say. Humour as sharp as Spike's relies heavily on this ability. What appears normal to us, is 'funny', i.e. not normal, to Spike. A typical piece of Milligan double think goes as follows:

> *Man: We ain't got no kids of our own.*
> *Interviewer: Whose kids have you got?*

Although most Horses are slow to anger, Spike Milligan is something of a thoroughbred, an exception who proves the rule. Highly sensitive, he kicks those who ride him badly. Throughout Spike's life, he has hit out angrily at all forms of petty officialdom and bureaucracy, especially when it touches him personally. His tantrums and rages have been directed at the BBC, BUPA, the GPO and countless others. My own wish is that Spike's often justifiable rages never cease. That he will have me weeping with laughter is beyond doubt.

Horses have great personality

Clint Eastwood

When you first discover the Chinese Horoscopes you may sometimes find yourself uncertain about your influences – there is a lot to take on board which is new. A useful tip is to refer to the actual animal itself, whose behaviour is a blue-print of our own. Of course, some animals of the Horoscope are more familiar than others. We seldom meet Snakes or Tigers in Britain, but everyone has met a Horse. You have only to watch a Clint Eastwood spaghetti western to see dozens. Indeed, I have always thought it highly appropriate that Hollywood's most popular cowboy was born in the Year of the Horse. Appropriate, and highly predictable within the laws of the Chinese Horoscope.

Clint Eastwood was born in California on May 31, 1930, and I can think of no public figure born in the Year of the Horse, and there are a great many, who better illustrates the Horse's practical nature. A child of the Big Depression, the young Clint Eastwood was taken by his father to wherever there was work. His father impressed on his son the philosophy of, 'you don't get something for nothing'. The boy took notice. Before his astonishing success in Hollywood, Clint Eastwood worked as a lumberjack, pumped gas and dug swimming pools. Horses are good with their hands, and not frightened of getting them dirty to earn a living. And it is the dominance of the Horse's practical skills that has done so much to elevate Clint Eastwood from a $75 dollar a week bit player to one of the world's highest paid stars (it is estimated that his films have grossed well over $1.5 billion dollars). The movie that proved the turning point, and considered by many to be one of his best was *The Outlaw Josey Wales*. He both acted the lead and directed it. The transition to actor/director, and later to producer, provided Clint Eastwood with a chance to display his Horse gifts to the full.

Although making movies is an art form, it remains essentially a job for practical people. Top movie directors need huge bags of energy to deal with the long arduous hours, and the hundreds of ever-changing problems that are part and parcel of shooting a film. The image of directors screaming at actors is false, and no one is less flappable than Clint Eastwood. A true Horse, he absorbs the frenzy of those around him, leading by the sheer weight of his personality. A colleague once said: 'As a leader, he doesn't want to look over his shoulder to see if the troops are following. He knows they are.'

Horses seldom express rage. But the Chinese say that once you have witnessed a raging Horse, you will never forget it. In keeping with the Horse influence, Clint Eastwood is no exception. But so far as one can tell, he only allows the dark rage that one senses lurking beneath his cool exterior for the camera. And when you examine it, Clint Eastwood's whole acting style has been based on pent-up anger exploding. His creation, Dirty Harry, is embodiment of rage reaching boiling point: 'Go on Punk. Make my day.' It says it all.

Further proof of the Horse in Clint Eastwood can be found in his huge output. Producing movies at an extraordinary rate, he once made four pictures, all box office successes, in just under seventeen months. He acted in, as well as directed two of them. To make movies that quickly, it is necessary to be organised and efficient. Eastwood is both, and knows it; Horses are not a little vain, it must be added. Moreover, he hates being part of any team. He is a leader, and says so. You can take it or leave it.

Today, Clint Eastwood combines Hollywood with the mayor's desk in his home town of Carmel, California. His hobbies, not that a Horse has much time for them, are hitting a golf ball and sharing a beer with a few guys in a downtown bar. Off screen he gives the impression of a man who is shy and self-effacing. But the truth is that no one gets to be as big as Clint Eastwood by *being* shy and self-effacing. What gets a man like Clint Eastwood to the top is having the good fortune to be born in the Year of the Horse.

Zola Budd

Each of the signs that make up the Chinese Horoscope are unique, but there is one sign more so – the Year of the Fire Horse. Occurring every sixty years, the Fire Horse brings with it a bag of mixed blessings. In Vietnam Fire Horse babies, especially girls, are actually considered as harbingers of bad fortune. It was at one time not uncommon to find Fire Horse girls utterly rejected by their parents. Some even died at their parent's hands. I mention this only to illustrate how seriously the East take their horoscope.

Sometimes terrible, sometimes a joy, the Fire Horse Year and all those born under its influence will never be overlooked. Certainly the tiny elfin figure of Zola Budd has had plenty of attention. Some might say too much. A typical Fire Horse, Zola Budd was born in South Africa on May 26, 1966. From the moment she first appeared on the international scene Zola Budd stormed into the headlines. No other athlete has aroused more public indignation since the black runner, Jesse Owens, upset Hitler's racist mob in Munich during the Olympic Games of 1936.

Yet at the same time, Zola Budd's critics have been fulsome in their praise of her undoubted gifts as an athlete, which are greatly enhanced by the Fire Horse's influence. It must be emphasised, however, that the Fire Horse does not possess different characteristics to an ordinary Horse person, it is simply that all the characteristics are amplified. Horses have enormous stamina; Fire Horses have it in abundance.

There can be few sights more compelling than a thoroughbred racehorse running at full stretch, and Zola Budd has inherited much of that particular quality. And once you get through the political web that has somehow kept her true personality in the dark, Zola Budd emerges as a bright, independent spirit – another strong Horse characteristic is independence. Ms Budd once underlined this point in a statement she made when she first arrived in Britain. 'I want simply to be able to run where I like,' she said, 'without interference.'

It is said that Fire Horse children will find their early years more difficult than most, and will seldom if ever establish lasting family ties. This would certainly seem the case of Zola Budd, whose relationship with her father broke down completely following, so it was alleged, a payment made by the *Daily Mail* during the period they were serialising Zola's life story. But the real reason, as those who know their Chinese Horoscopes will tell you is that the Fire Horse kicks down the paddock door just as soon as they have the strength. Of all the headlines created as a result of Zola Budd's arrival, none captures the Fire Horse influence better than those that followed her race against Mary Decker. The Olympic games of 1984 were held in the year of the Rat, a sign that does not favour Horses. It doesn't favour Dogs either – Mary Decker was born on August 4, 1958. The race in which Miss Decker fell crashing to the ground, her agonised expression and Zola Budd's utter bewilderment has left a deep impression on all those who saw it. The promise of great things, and the disastrous reality are just two extremes of the Fire Horse influence.

In terms of Zola Budd's future, we have to look no further than the Horse's mouth. With the good common sense of Horse people everywhere, she says simply, 'Give me time.' And time, it must be said, is on her side. The next five-star Horse year is in 1991 – the year of the Goat. By then, Zola Budd will be twenty-five, with her best running at its peak. Even so, it is perhaps in the nature of the Fire Horse that the crucial Olympic games nearest the Goat year is 1992; just one year too late.

Chrissie and John Lloyd (both Horses)

The Chinese Horoscope says, with some emphasis, that it is not advisable for two animals of the same sign to marry. There are exceptions; Cats and Pigs, for example, and there are some signs which are on the border. Of these, the Horse is typical. Two Horses *can* get together, but whatever they do, first of all their boundaries have to be clearly defined. Horses are deeply independent, and baulk from any restriction in their need to move as they wish. Marriage very often creates restrictions. And whereas two Horses share much in common to cement ties, there is more in their influencing sign to tear them apart. You have only to examine the highly publicised marriage, separation and divorce, of Chris Evert and John Lloyd, to see what I mean.

Chris Evert was born in Fort Lauderdale, Southern Florida on December 21, 1954. Her background was tennis from the very start. 'When I was a child,' she once observed, 'I had three pairs of shoes – school shoes, Sunday shoes and tennis shoes.' She might have added horse shoes, for there were long hours of practice. Her father threw balls, and the young Chrissie hit them back. Deprived of her share of childhood fun, Chrissie put her energies into perfecting her skills. The Horse character is never more at home than when applying their gifts of endurance and practicality. More recently, of course, we have seen Chrissie's practical nature extend beyond the tennis court. As a result of careful investments and endorsements, Chrissie has earned millions of dollars.

John Lloyd was born in Leigh-on-Sea, near Southend, Essex, on August 27, 1954. His family were also tennis orientated. All three Lloyd sons represented Britain in the Davis Cup. Clearly, in the face of his wife's success, it is not easy to judge John's achievements as a player. Whatever they may be, there is a large school of thought which says that John Lloyd would have been a far better player if he had enjoyed an American style of coaching. He certainly didn't lack the talent.

However, although we may speculate on John's missed opportunity and Chrissie's tough future, the fact remains that they are a pair of strong-minded Horses. They married, played the same sport, and made news. Their private life was as exposed as a Wimbledon final and got almost as much media attention.

Before her marriage, Chrissie had led a typical Horse life, filling it with near perfection on the court, and spending her off-court time with an interesting collection of box office beefcake. As well as Jimmy Connors, whom she'd been engaged to, Chrissie hung on the arms of Vitas Gerulaitus, Jack Ford and Burt Reynolds. Although her looks are not exactly fashion-plate, Chrissie's tanned, firm limbs, and high-powered personality are seductive weapons. John, on the other hand, has the classic English appearance, and his pre-marital days saw a string of starlets pass through his meadow. They included Maureen Nolan, of the singing Nolan Sisters.

Whereas a Horse might endure any degree of pressure caused by work, romance presents a problem for the graceful, elegant, equine personality. Horses are practical at heart, and love throws no lifebelts for the practically minded. The Lloyds separated in 1984, the year of the somewhat unstable Rat. It looked then as if their marriage was beyond saving. But tennis players have a knack of fighting back, and they got back together again. However, for once their Horse stamina did not last. In 1987 they finally got divorced.

Horses quickly become bored and constantly take up new interests

Famous Horses

Sports
Mike Brearley
Chris Evert
Jack Hobbs
John Lloyd
Doug Mountjoy
Brough Scott
Freddie Trueman

Royalty
Princess Margaret
Lord Snowdon

Arts
Leonard Bernstein
Sir John Betjeman
Frederick Chopin
Puccini
Rembrandt

Media
Rowan Atkinson
Lionel Bart
Tony Blackburn
Claire Bloom
Ray Charles
Ronnie Corbett
Sean Connery
Billy Connolly

James Dean
Clint Eastwood
Samantha Fox
Lew Grade
Larry Grayson
Jimi Hendrix
Bob Hoskins
Paul McCartney
Spike Milligan
Alan Price
Barbra Streisand
King Vidor
Joanne Woodwood

Politics
Neil Kinnock
Lenin
Willie Whitelaw
Shirley Williams

Literature
J. B. Priestley

Others
Neil Armstrong
Michael Edwardes
Billy Graham
Tiny Rowland

A Special Word on Compatibility

Throughout this book I have done my best to translate the Chinese view of compatibility with that of our own. But there are distinct differences between our two cultures which need clarification.

For the Chinese, love is seldom seen as something separate from marriage, an experience to be enjoyed in isolation. It is seen as part of a natural progression. In other words, love and marriage are thought of as a whole, and in this context their system of grading the compatibility of animal signs makes a lot of sense. In the West, if we have a love affair, we do so aware that it might or might not work out. In China that is not the case; there a couple find love later, accepting marriage as a kind of business relationship which is impossible to dissolve, no matter what. In China, it is imperative, therefore, that a Dragon, say, should marry a Rat, Rooster or Monkey; a Horse should marry a Goat, and a Dog should marry a Tiger.

But whatever your choice, the compatibility charts should not be read like the Ten Commandments, and not taken as law. They are more akin to a 'Good Food Guide'. We often enjoy meals in places with no stars, and are disappointed by five-star restaurants. It is the same with compatibility. If your partner is zero rated, but you love them, that's fine.

What the charts do, however, is prepare you for the future. Few people know what to expect when they embark on a new relationship. The changes that take place when a relationship develops badly are those we have all experienced; a sense of surprise followed by a sense of frustration. 'If only I had known this or that about him, or her', is a more than familiar expression, one we have almost certainly used ourselves. Quite simply, the job of the compatibility charts is to take the sting out of such a process. To be warned is to be prepared.

Above all, the compatibility charts provide a choice, saying if you want a relationship that is tailor made then here are the candidates. And if you want to put your money on an outsider, then it's up to you. But in any event, it must be emphasised that the compatibility charts are not carved in stone. At the same time, it is also worth remembering that they have been in existence for thousands of years. That they have stood the test of time, is, I believe, a tribute to their effectiveness.

Famous Horse Pairs, Couples and Groups

Simon and Garfunkel   (Snake)
Prince Michael of Kent and Princess Michael   (Rooster)
Duke of Windsor and Mrs Simpson   (Monkey)
Princess Margaret and Lord Snowdon   (both Horses)
Paul McCartney and George Harrison   (Goat)
John Lennon   (Dragon)
Ringo Starr   (Dragon)

Find Your Partner's and Friends' Animal Signs

Matt Sept 72

The Rat

1900	January 31st to February 18th	1901
1912	February 18th to February 5th	1913
1924	February 5th to January 23rd	1925
1936	January 24th to February 10th	1937
1948	February 10th to January 28th	1949
1960	January 28th to February 14th	1961
1972	January 15th to February 2nd	1973
1984	February 2nd to February 19th	1985

The Buffalo

1901	February 19th to February 7th	1902
1913	February 6th to January 25th	1914
1925	January 24th to February 12th	1926
1937	February 11th to January 30th	1938
1949	January 29th to February 16th	1950
1961	February 15th to February 4th	1962
1973	February 3rd to January 22nd	1974
1985	February 20th to February 8th	1986

The Tiger

1902	February 8th to January 28th	1903
1914	January 26th to February 13th	1915
1926	February 13th to February 1st	1927
1938	January 31st to February 18th	1939
1950	February 17th to February 5th	1951
1962	February 5th to January 24th	1963
1974	January 23rd to February 10th	1975
1986	February 9th to January 28th	1987

The Cat

1903	January 29th to February 15th	1904
1915	February 14th to February 2nd	1916
1927	February 2nd to January 22nd	1928
1939	February 19th to February 7th	1940
1951	February 6th to January 26th	1952
1963	January 25th to February 12th	1964
1975	February 11th to January 30th	1976
1987	January 29th to February 16th	1988

The Dragon

1904	February 16th to February 3rd	1905
1916	February 3rd to January 22nd	1917
1928	January 23rd to February 9th	1929
1940	February 8th to January 26th	1941
1952	January 27th to February 13th	1953
1964	February 13th to February 1st	1965
1976	January 31st to February 17th	1977
1988	February 17th to February 5th	1989

The Snake

1905	February 4th to January 24th	1906
1917	January 23rd to February 10th	1918
1929	February 10th to January 29th	1930
1941	January 27th to February 14th	1942
1953	February 14th to February 2nd	1954
1965	February 2nd to January 20th	1966
1977	February 18th to February 6th	1978
1989	February 6th to January 26th	1990

The Goat

1907	February 13th to February 1st	1908
1919	February 1st to February 19th	1920
1931	February 17th to February 5th	1932
1943	February 5th to January 24th	1944
1955	January 24th to February 11th	1956
1967	February 9th to January 29th	1968
1979	January 28th to February 15th	1980

The Monkey

1908	February 2nd to January 21st	1909
1920	February 20th to February 7th	1921
1932	February 6th to January 25th	1933
1944	January 25th to February 12th	1945
1956	February 12th to January 30th	1957
1968	January 30th to February 16th	1969
1980	February 16th to February 4th	1981

Jon Oct. 69

The Rooster

1909	January 22nd	to	February 9th	1910
1921	February 8th	to	January 27th	1922
1933	January 26th	to	February 13th	1934
1945	February 13th	to	February 1st	1946
1957	January 31st	to	February 17th	1958
1969	February 17th	to	February 5th	1970
1981	February 5th	to	January 24th	1982

The Dog

1910	February 10th	to	January 29th	1911
1922	January 28th	to	February 15th	1923
1934	February 14th	to	February 3rd	1935
1946	February 2nd	to	January 21st	1947
1958	February 18th	to	February 7th	1959
1970	February 6th	to	January 26th	1971
1982	January 25th	to	February 12th	1983

The Pig

1911	January 30th to February 17th	1912
1923	February 16th to February 4th	1924
1935	February 4th to January 23rd	1936
1947	January 22nd to February 9th	1948
1959	February 8th to January 27th	1960
1971	January 27th to February 14th	1972
1983	February 13th to February 1st	1984

A Brief Look at the Other Animal Signs

The Rat

The Rat is born under the sign of charm. Rats are warm, passionate and the supreme opportunist. They live for the day and seldom plan for tomorrow. Time does not concern them. Rats have sharp wits and an eye for detail, which favours them if they choose to become writers. Rats make excellent critics and salesmen. However, Rats have an undercurrent of aggression which occasionally expresses itself in worrying over details. In extreme cases, some Rats undergo a complete reversal and become obsessed by making plans and keeping statistics. Such Rats should not be rubbed up the wrong way. All Rats are devoted and love their family. They care little about their surroundings and are uncomplicated in affairs of the heart. Rats make money, but they cannot hold on to it. Rats love to scheme. They have a tendency to grumble when things go wrong.

The Buffalo

The Buffalo is born under the twin signs of equilibrium and tenacity. Buffalo people are conservative with a big and small

C, even if they hide behind a façade of being Left Wing. They work exceptionally hard and are strong and resolute in their business dealings. As parents they are firm and authoritative. Buffaloes are great achievers and feature prominently on the World Stage. They do not suffer fools, but find self criticism difficult. Buffaloes are stubborn and reliable, but they have complex hearts. In matters of romance they are often all at sea, seldom building lasting relationships. When a Buffalo has a conviction, he makes it the centrepiece of his life. Without conviction, a Buffalo can easily go to seed. Buffaloes do not care to share power. They love tradition and gardening.

The Tiger

Tigers are born under the sign of courage. They are brave, powerful people with a strong sense of their personal identity. They are natural revolutionaries and are disrespectful of authority. Tigers are quick tempered, and will risk everything for any cause that they believe in. This is particularly true of a Tiger in love. Tigers are great on ideas, seeming to possess a never-ending stream of original schemes. But the Tiger is a short paced creature and after a fast start, they are likely to run out of breath. They love to be the boss figure, usually ending up in charge of a team. The Tiger's life is often full of danger, and Tigers live life to the full. This sometimes means that a Tiger will meet a tragic and sudden end. Most of all, a Tiger needs to become fully himself, no matter what the cost. In other words, a Tiger needs to show the world what they are made of. They are very generous.

The Cat

Cats are born under the sign of virtue. They are social and refined with a good nose for bargains. Cats have good manners, good taste and place a high premium on family life. They are methodical, sometimes obsessively so. Cats are extremely diplomatic and are good listeners. Not original, Cats nevertheless show a great appreciation of beauty. They have shrewd artistic judgement and are acquisitive. Once a Cat has struck a deal he will keep it, come what may. Some Cats become ruthless when given power beyond their capability, but they are not normally concerned with matters outside domestic life. Cats hate change in routine and are sometimes a bit snobbish. Cats respond poorly to pressure, and will cave in emotionally under stress. A Cat's advice is well intentioned. They take their time when coming to a decision, and are very sensuous. All Cats dress well.

The Dragon

Dragons are born under the sign of luck. They are the national symbol of China and are believed to bring the three great eastern benedictions: wealth, long life and harmony. Dragons often become national heroes and have a magnetic personality. They are loved by many, but seldom love deeply in return. Dragons are impulsive, hot-headed and strive relentlessly for perfection. They have big hearts, broad interests and their advice is very wise. Dragons offer both their wisdom and professions of love freely and often. Dragons are generous, but often let their hearts rule their heads. Once they have begun a task, they see it through, regardless of its merit. Forced into a corner, the Dragon makes a poor judge and an even worse diplomat. They hate routine. Full of self-confidence, the Dragon can achieve anything.

The Snake

Snakes are born under the sign of wisdom. Guided by intuition, Snakes are wise, intelligent and think deeply. Snakes have a restless intellect which causes them to change direction many times in life. Although they do not give up easily, Snakes go through long periods of inactivity. This usually happens before a major change. Snakes are poor gamblers, and when asked to decide quickly, often make the wrong decision. They are possessive in human relationships and cling to those they love. Snakes are both peaceful and artistic, and have the gifts of music and humour. They are also capable of great artistic innovation. Snake women have the power to bewitch. Unlucky in love, Snakes can make a lot of money when they need to, and can become extremely wealthy. Snakes don't give up.

The Goat

The Goat is born under the sign of art, and as their sign suggests love all things beautiful. Goats are society's peacemakers and adore good company. They love the *dolce vita* and are usually acquisitive. Goats pay a lot of attention to their homes and maintain strong family ties. They have, however, a capricious side to their nature which expresses itself most notably in a fickle heart. Goats are fine hosts and generous to their friends. Although they excel in all branches of the arts, they do not make good businessmen. Goats often overstate their case, or chose the wrong moment to make a point. Goats do better when not left to initiate the first move. Once tethered, so to speak, Goats may become extremely successful. A Goat's views are often superficial, influenced by trend. Thoughtful and amusing, the Goat's main problem is coming to terms with his natural waywardness.

The Monkey

Monkeys are born under the sign of fantasy. They are highly intelligent, active, and capable of turning their abundant skills to any use they choose. Above all, the Monkey has the power to win others over to his way of thinking. This they do by a mixture of art and craft. Talkative, humorous, with agile if somewhat imitative minds, Monkeys have a thirst for knowledge and new experiences. But Monkeys have a rather high opinion of themselves, and they are often superficial in their judgement of others. Monkeys are first class wheeler-dealers. They are careful with money, and it happens that they always make plenty. Monkeys are acquisitive and have wonderful memories. They are excellent organisers, but are easily seduced in affairs of the heart. Long-term relationships often elude the Monkey. In spite of the fact that Monkeys have few scruples, they care a great deal about their children. Monkeys will try anything once.

The Rooster

The Rooster is born under the sign of candour. They speak their minds frankly and openly, and always truthfully. They are deeply conservative, orderly in their daily lives, but have a boastful manner. Never short of an opinion, Roosters are sociable and spend much of their time dreaming up schemes which seldom bear fruit. In matters of finance, Roosters are either thrifty or spendthrifts; nothing in between. They are keen gardeners and adore home life. Successful in business, Roosters love the limelight, but they lack initiative and are best in partnership. Although they like to dress up and put on a show, Roosters are old fashioned in affairs of the heart. Roosters are honest, talkative and incorruptible. They regard their love life as strictly private and hold moral views on all matters. Roosters born between the hours of 5 and 7 are the most vocal. Lacking tact, Roosters are models of generosity. All Roosters are methodical.

The Dog

Dogs are born under the sign of loyalty. All Dogs are faithful, with warm hearts and a touchingly honest approach to everything they do. Dogs frequently find themselves defending those less fortunate and are just in their judgements. They fight bravely when roused, but have a tendency to act stubbornly. Dogs are practical in business but dither in the face of romance. Once set a worthwhile task, a Dog will never give up. They are watchful and often argumentative. The

Dog's big problem is his constant anxiety. All Dogs suffer from an inability to stop worrying over details. They are occasionally blunt in their public dealings, but are easy going and delightful when in the company of friends. Dogs are good to their parents and never hypocritical. If he can tell the wood from the trees, a Dog will be a success. Dogs who have suffered bad experiences should be avoided. Dog women are often very vivacious.

The Pig

The Pig is born under the sign of honesty. Pigs are hard working and fun loving. Pigs enjoy all forms of social life and throw themselves into both work and leisure with great gusto. Big hearted, Pigs are jovial and forthright. They are lucky in business and seem to be able to make money whenever they want. In the matters of romance, Pigs are straightforward and direct; they are not ones for sophisticated courtship. Well informed and robust in character, the Pig is dependable and organises his life to suit himself. Sometimes the Pig has too high an opinion of his worth. Here he can be duped in his financial affairs or jilted in romance. Pigs adore their family and are generous with invitations to their homes. Slow to anger, Pigs are sometimes too gossipy for their own good. Men Pigs are often fancy dressers. Pigs are best in partnerships.

Author's Note

The year of the Cat

Is it the year of the Cat, Rabbit or Hare? On the surface it is all a bit confusing, but there is a very simple explanation. The name you adopt depends very largely on which part of the world you come from. This is how it works.

Although it is true to say that the Chinese invented their wonderful horoscope, they are not the only ones who use it. During the 2,000 years it has been in existence the Chinese Horoscope has now travelled around the world. But if the horoscopes are new to us in the West, they have been with the nations close to China since the very start – well, almost. Not unnaturally each new country refined the twelve animal signs of the horoscope to suit themselves, to fit in with their particular culture. For instance, the people of Hong Kong name what the Chinese call the Rabbit, the Hare. In Vietnam, Cambodia and Korea, the Rabbit is called the Cat. The reason is simple. These people consider the word 'Rabbit' an insult. Likewise, many Chinese are offended at being termed a Cat.

My own researches show that the very first written word for the Cat/Rabbit/Hare year was, in Chinese, a 'creature with soft fur and a weak back'. Clearly it is a description which can easily fit all three animals.

Curiously the West did not learn about the Chinese Horoscopes from the Chinese, but from the Vietnamese who settled in France following the Indochinese war in the 50s. This is why so many Westerners call the years 1903, 1915, 1927, 1939, 1951, 1963, 1975 and 1987 the Year of the Cat.

But the most important point of all is to remember that all the experts agree that no matter what the word – Cat, Rabbit or Hare, the influence is *exactly the same!*

Also, the Rooster is sometimes called the Cock, the Buffalo the Ox, the Goat the Sheep and the Pig the Boar.

The author is grateful to the following reference sources for additional material:

Chinese Horoscopes by Paula Delsol, (Pan)
The Way to Chinese Astrology: the Four Pillars of Wisdom Jean-Michel Huon de Kermadec, (Unwin)
The Handbook of Chinese Horoscopes Theodora Lau, (Arrow).